I0626934

MALCOLM X IN GAZA:
A COLORING BOOK
ILLUSTRATED BY NATHI NGUBANE

Note to the parents and teachers—

This year marks one hundred years since Malcolm X, the fiery revolutionary, thinker, and activist was born in the United States of America.

As we witness a time of genocide and ethnic cleansing in Palestine, a protracted civil war and foreign interference in Sudan, as well as rising authoritarianism in several parts of the globe and a devaluing of our humanity everywhere, Malcolm's journey as a thinker and activist is perhaps instructive to this moment.

Over the years, much has been written about Malcolm's journey from a young man who engaged in petty crime, to his rapid rise within the Black nationalist group, the Nation of Islam, and finally to his embrace of mainstream Sunni Islam. His is a story of redemption and revolution.

But not enough has been written about his time in Africa and the Middle East, especially Palestine. It's almost forgotten that Malcolm spent around six months on the continent and the Middle East in 1964, during which he completed Hajj before meeting a string of intellectuals, activists, and political leaders to call upon their advice and assistance in combating American racism. While he was welcomed wherever he went, he found it hard to find backers to take on the United States empire.

With Malcolm more relevant than ever, it is crucial to revisit his travels that were fundamental to his global legacy.

The stories in this book draw from a variety of sources on Malcolm X, including his biography and his little-known travel diary of 1964. But some of the more stunning details of his visit was derived from the memoirs of the famed Palestinian poet, Harun Hashim Rashid, who spent time with Malcolm in Gaza. These details were generously passed on to us by the Palestinian academic Jehad Abusalim.

The illustrations in this book are based on some of the photographs from the time, as well as Nathi's interpretation of Malcolm's interactions based on the evidence we have.

The idea behind this book is to extend the legacy of his internationalist, revolutionary thought to this crucial moment in world history. It was Malcolm who saw and spoke openly about the double standards of the United States. It was Malcolm who called for alliances in the fight against the thuggery of the liberal world order.

It's easy to venerate Malcolm's brave ideas, but how do we create a new generation of brave thinkers, willing to go to the ends of the earth to test their own understanding of the world?

We hope *Malcolm X in Gaza: A Coloring Book* will provide an introduction to that journey.

Azad Essa, Publisher
New York, May 2025

A BLACK MUSLIM ICON IS BORN

His name was Malcolm Little. On May 19, 1925, in the town of Omaha, Nebraska, Earl and Louise Little were blessed with a baby boy they named Malcolm. He was one of five children.

His father Earl, a priest and *activist* at the local church, died under mysterious circumstances when he was very young. Malcolm's mother, Louise, suffered from a long illness resulting in Malcolm being moved to a *foster home*.

Malcolm had a tough childhood in which he faced poverty and *racism* from *white supremacists* in the town.

As a young man, Malcolm often found himself in trouble. One day he was caught stealing and he was sent to prison.

In jail, he discovered a group called the Nation of Islam. The group opened his mind to new thoughts and ideas about the world.

Malcolm was so impressed with their ideas that he *converted* to Islam. He also changed his name from Malcolm Little to Malcolm X, to symbolize the rejection of his slave name and a connection to his unknown African ancestry.

WORDS TO LEARN

Activist	Someone who works hard to make the world a better place
Foster home	A place for children to live when they can no longer stay with their own family
Racism	A system in which people are treated badly or unfairly because of the color of their skin
White supremacists	People who believe that white people are superior to others
Converted	When someone changes their belief or religion to a new one

WELCOME TO OMAHA, NEBRASKA

LOUISE LITTLE

MALCOLM LITTLE

EARL LITTLE

THE REVOLUTIONARY

Malcolm entered prison as a *petty thief* but he left as a *revolutionary.*

He became an inspiring *preacher* and a *freedom fighter* who stood for the liberation of Black people in America.

But Malcolm was interested in helping all people, even beyond the United States.

He saw the difficulties faced by all *oppressed* people around the world as the same.

And because he always loved to learn, he traveled to countries in Africa and the Middle East to search for ways to fix the problems faced by the poor and the oppressed.

WORDS TO LEARN

Petty thief	A person who steals something of little value
Revolutionary	A person who dedicates their life to changing the world and helps others to do the same
Preacher	A religious leader
Freedom fighter	A person who stands up to an oppressive political or social system
Oppressed	People who are treated badly, or have their rights taken away from them

A TRAVELER

Malcolm loved to take photos of the places he visited.

In the summer of 1959, Malcolm traveled to Nigeria and Egypt.

In Sudan, he visited the **ancient city** of Omdurman where he was told about the **Nubian civilization**.

Later that year he went to Ghana, Syria, Saudi Arabia, and Palestine.

Wherever Malcolm went, he took photos and wrote in his diary. He was amazed by the stories of the past and the beliefs and the values of the people he met.

He felt **blessed** to meet with people of different backgrounds. He believed it made his life richer.

Wherever Malcolm went, he was treated with **respect** and warmth.

WORDS TO LEARN

Ancient city	A very old place where people lived and worked
Nubian civilization	An ancient civilization that existed alongside the Nile River in what is today southern Egypt and northern Sudan
Civilization	A group of people who live together and share a common way of life, culture, and beliefs
Blessed	To feel happy and lucky
Respect	To treat someone with love and care

MALCOLM GOES FOR HAJJ

Malcolm was not done discovering and learning about the world.

In the spirit of exploring Islam more fully, he went to Saudi Arabia in 1964 to complete the *Hajj* in Mecca.

Malcolm said the *brotherhood* he felt during Hajj left him "speechless." He took on a new name, too: El-Hajj Malik El-Shabazz.

After Mecca, he sought out more adventure.

Malcolm returned to Sudan, Ghana and Nigeria but also traveled to Lebanon, Ethiopia, Kenya and Tanzania, Liberia, Guinea, and Algeria.

In Ghana, he met some great leaders, like Kwame Nkrumah, the first prime minister and president of the country.

He said that all the visits and the people he met along the way made his soul bigger.

Malcolm was so comfortable in the countries in Africa and the Middle East, he said leaving the United States felt as if he had stepped out of a prison.

And then Malcolm went to Gaza.

WORDS TO LEARN

Hajj	A spiritual journey Muslims must try to make once in their life to their holy city, Mecca
Brotherhood	A feeling of closeness, or support, and understanding between people

RETURN TO PALESTINE

Malcolm had a special place in his heart for Palestine.

When he landed in Gaza on September 5, 1964, he was welcomed by Muhammad Khulusi Bseiso, a famous Palestinian judge and *scholar*.

Malcolm prayed in the old mosques of Gaza, walked through busy markets, and saw famous *textiles* and pottery.

He was amazed by the *orange groves* and the apricot trees.

He loved seeing it all.

WORDS TO LEARN

Scholar	A person who has much knowledge, usually acquired from research and study
Textiles	Different types of cloth like shirts, dresses, towels, and blankets
Orange groves	A family of orange trees

VISITING KHAN YOUNIS

Gaza was also a place with a lot of pain.

Many hundreds of thousands of Palestinians lived in Gaza as *refugees* after they were pushed out of their homes in other parts of Palestine when Israel became a country in 1948.

This is known as the Al-Nakba, or the *catastrophe*.

Malcolm took time to visit the Khan Younis *refugee camp*, one of eight camps that were built for Palestinians in Gaza.

The camps were overflowing with people who had lost their homes. There were not enough schools, clean water, or medicines.

It broke Malcolm's heart to hear the stories of the families. But Malcolm was amazed by how strong the people remained.

WORDS TO LEARN

Refugee	Someone who has to escape their home country because of war or oppression
Catastrophe	When something happens that hurts a lot of people and changes their lives forever
Refugee camp	A temporary living area for people who had to escape their home country because it was no longer safe to live there

MEETING A POET

Malcolm was brilliant with words. And he loved poetry, too!

In Gaza, Malcolm met a famous Palestinian *poet*, Harun Hashem Rashid. Harun showed him around and helped him understand all the challenges people were facing.

The poet Rashid said that Malcolm had tears in his eyes when he heard about how Israel had murdered so many people in Gaza.

Malcolm was so *determined* to let the world know about his support for the Palestinians, he scribbled down Rashid's poem into his diary:

We must return
No boundaries should exist
No obstacles can stop us
Cry out refugees: "We shall return"
Tell the Mts: "We shall return"
Tell the alley: "We shall return"
We are going back to our youth

Palestine calls us to arm ourselves
And we are armed and are going to fight
We must return

—Harun Hashem Rashid

WORDS TO LEARN

Poet	A person who uses words to tell imaginative songs and stories
Determined	When you don't give up on a job or a task or a project

18

THE RELIGIOUS LEADERS OF GAZA

Malcolm prayed in Gaza.

After a long day of meetings and discussions, Malcolm spent time with the religious leaders of Gaza.

Later, he prayed Isha, the evening prayer with them.

After prayer, he was taken to the **parliament building** in Gaza, where he spoke with journalists.

Many people came to see Malcolm and presented him with gifts as a way to show their **gratitude** for visiting and caring about them.

Later that night, before he went to sleep, Malcolm wrote in his diary: "At 8:25 p.m. we left for the mosque to pray with several religious leaders. The spirit of **Allah** was strong."

WORDS TO LEARN

Parliament building	A building where leaders meet to make decisions for the people
Gratitude	Feeling happy and thankful for something good that happened or something someone did
Allah	The Arabic word for God

MALCOLM'S PROMISE

The next day, when the sun hit the highest point in the sky, Malcolm left for Cairo.

Judge Bseiso personally took Malcolm to the Arish airport to say goodbye to him.

As Malcolm climbed the stairs of the plane, he looked at the crowd and waved goodbye.

"We shall return! We shall return!" he said.

Although Malcolm's trip to Gaza was short, he was forever changed by the *experience.*

In the days after his visit to Gaza, Malcolm spoke and wrote more about the oppression faced by the Palestinian people.

WORDS TO LEARN

Experience — When the things you see or hear or feel helps shape how you think about something

A LEGACY TO REMEMBER

When he returned to the United States in December 1964, Malcolm was a changed man.

"I, for one, would like to impress, especially upon those who call themselves leaders, the importance in realizing the direct connection between the struggle of the Afro-American in this country and the struggle of our people all over the world," Malcolm said.

On February 21, 1965, Malcolm was **assassinated** in New York City.

His ideas had become too dangerous for the powerful. But like all **martyrs**, his struggle and cause for **justice** lived on in America and across the world, including Gaza.

Malcolm influenced Palestinian writers and thinkers like Edward Said and Refaat Alareer.

Malcolm left us, but his ideas and **legacy** live on in our fight for liberation.

WORDS TO KNOW

Assassinated	When someone is targeted and killed for political reasons
Justice	To treat people equally and with fairness
Martyr	Someone who sacrifices their life for a greater cause
Legacy	The ideas, things, and dreams a person leaves behind when they pass away

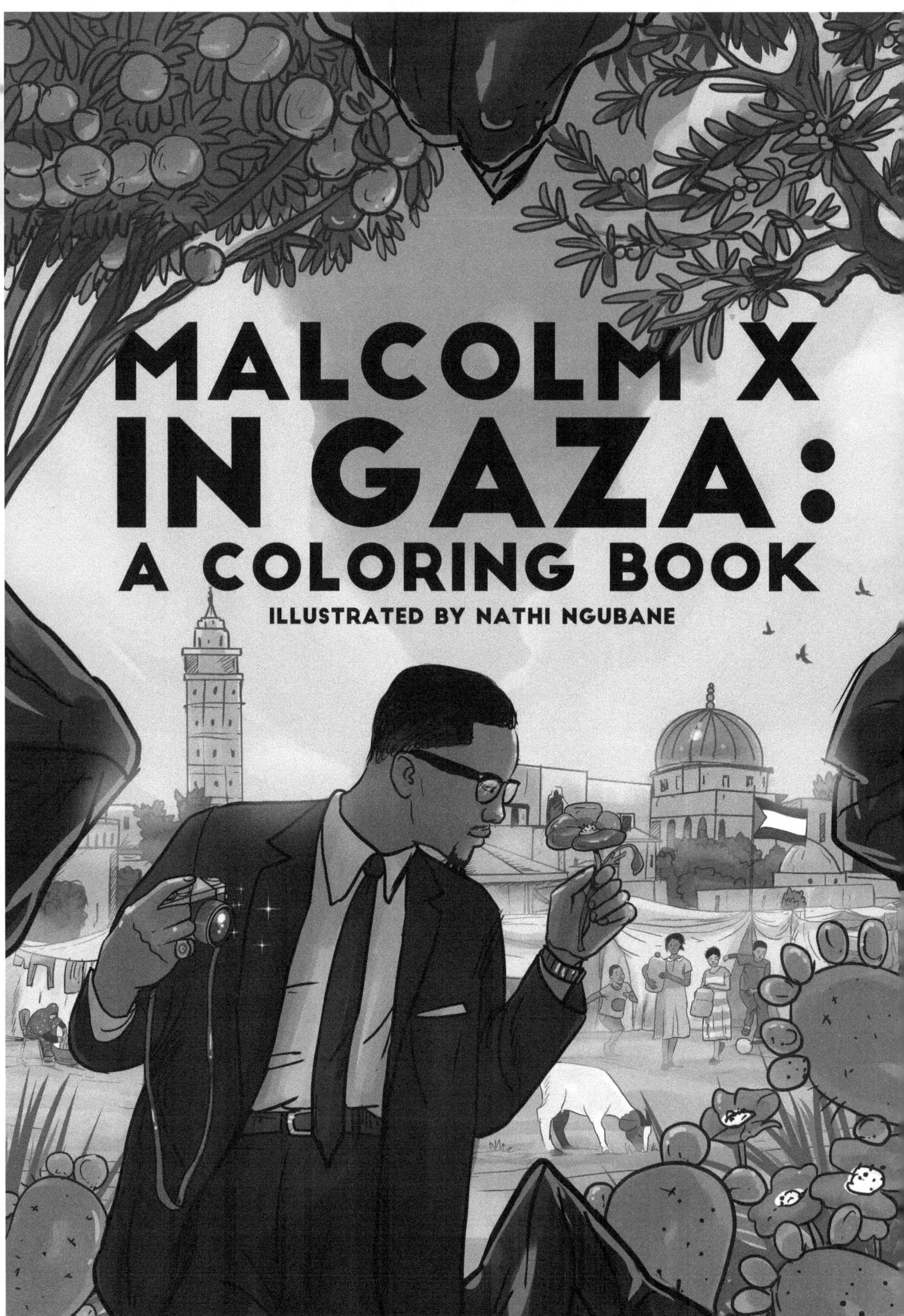

About the cover

The *Malcolm X in Gaza* cover draws inspiration from his iconic 1964 image, where he gazes out a home window while holding an M1 Carbine rifle as he faced a threat to his life. My reimagining replaces the rifle with a camera, capturing Malcolm as he prepares to photograph a Palestinian poppy—a tribute to his passion for photography and his love for Palestine.

This book traces his visit to Africa and the Middle East and imagines what he may have seen during his encounters and discoveries on his travels.

Staying true to the theme of the first coloring book, *From the River to the Sea*, I've brought back symbols of Palestine: the cactus, poppy, Jaffa oranges, Dome of the Rock and olive trees. Behind Malcolm, there is a snapshot the Khan Younis refugee camp, with the children of Gaza playing freely—a symbol of hope and liberation. Look closely, and you'll notice the rocks surrounding Malcolm form an "X", a subtle yet powerful nod to his long lasting influence.

Malcolm X was a champion of human rights. He was a fearless activist whose legacy continues to inspire generations today.

Nathi Ngubane, Illustrator

Acknowledgements

From start to end, our projects are a community effort.

And like our first coloring book, *From the River to the Sea: A Colouring Book*, this project was crowdfunded and only made possible by the generous support of friends and artists and well-wishers around the world.

We remain committed to creating a portfolio of alternate educational material for children (and adults) that is both accessible and affordable.

To this end we would like to thank the following people for coming forward with their support and timely input as we raced to complete this project in time for the centenary:

Jehad Abusalim, Aisha Adawiya, Siraj Ahmed, Leena Alarian, Kavita Algu, Nagla Bedir, Saif Khalid, Hafsa Kanjwal, Yousuf Kanjwal, Javeria Ahmad, Ebrahim Essa, Rooksana Essa, Shenaaz Essa, Aasiya Hassan, Hamza Hassan, Raheel Hassan, Fawzia Syed, Zaineb Haider, Aamnah Khan, Samee Ahmad, and many others.

We are thrilled to be once again collaborating with 1804 Books and we are grateful to Layan Fuleihan and Kate Gonzales for their warmth and belief in the project.

As always, if you are interested in collaborating, or providing support for our work, do get in touch.

We would love to hear from you. In solidarity,

Azad Essa, Sarwat Malik (US campaign manager), Sameera Essa (SA campaign manager), Gulshan Khan (editor and designer), & Nathi Ngubane (illustrator)

Social Bandit Media is a media collective based between Johannesburg and New York City. It was established in 2018.

To learn more: www.socialbanditmedia.co.za or connect with us on Instagram: @socialbanditmedia

About the author

Nathi Ngubane is a South African-based writer and illustrator. He grew up in Chesterville, a small township in Durban, KZN. After graduating with a diploma in Graphic Design from The Durban University of Technology, he landed his first freelance gig as a political cartoonist for *The Daily Vox* . In 2015, he was approached by *The Citizen News* with a position in political cartooning. In 2018, he resigned to focus on his brand, Think Ahead Comix.

His first children's book, *Duma Says: Wash Your Hands, Wear a Mask!* was published in 2020, followed by *Duma Says: Let's Live!* , a collector's edition with two more stories in the series. In August 2021, he released his latest book in the series titled *Duma Says: Your ABCs to Good Health* . His most recent coloring book, *From the River to the Sea,* was published in 2024 and was a national bestseller in South Africa. It has sold 18,000 copies worldwide. His work has also been featured on *Al Jazeera* , *BBC* , *Daily Maverick* , *New Frame* , & others.

Also from Social Bandit Media...

FROM THE RIVER TO THE SEA:
A Colouring Book

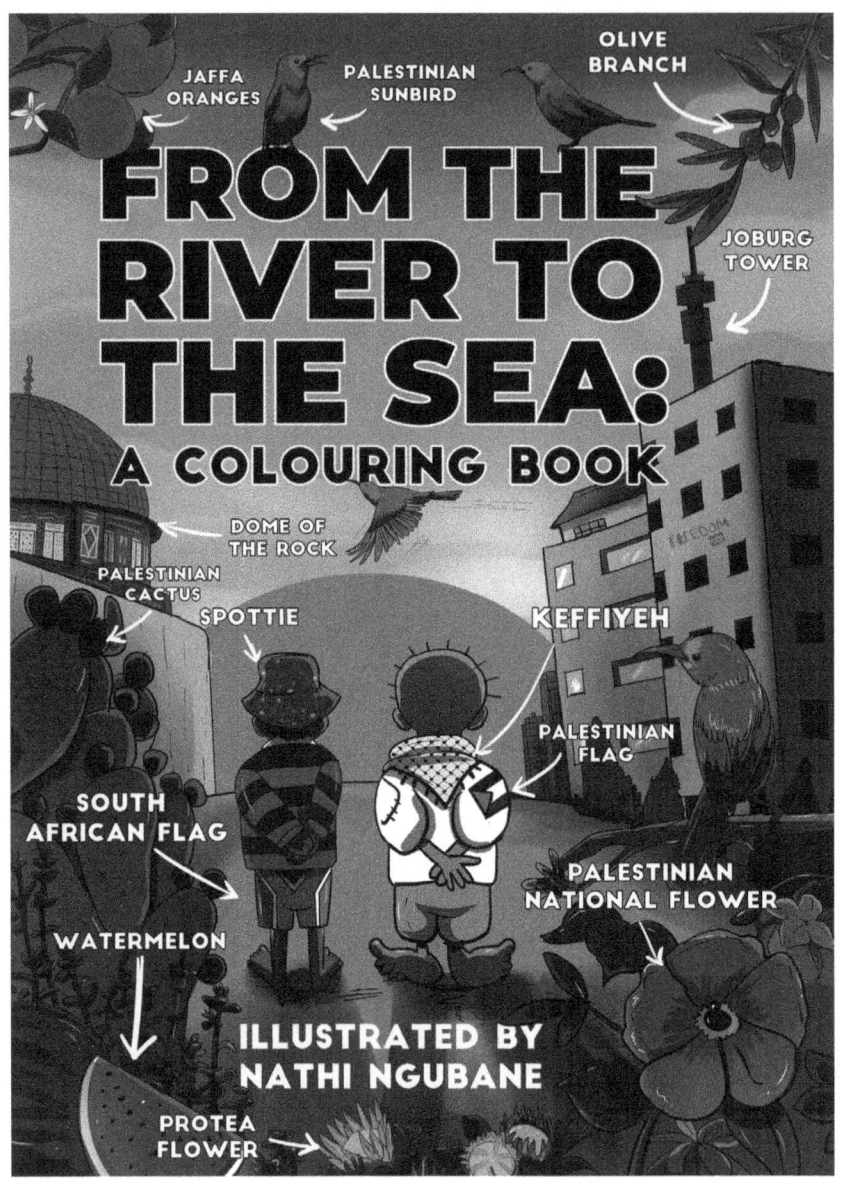

From the River to the Sea is an educational coloring book that provides a gateway into the story of Palestine. Through a series of stunning illustrations, Soweto-based Nathi Ngubane, tackles the injustice of the Nakba, delves into the history and culture of the land, and introduces young readers to the key concepts driving and sustaining Palestinian resistance.

www.ingramcontent.com/pod-product-compliance
Lightning Source LLC
Chambersburg PA
CBHW041533110626
46530CB00043B/605